C000055498

Thomas Merton

Contemplative and Peace-maker

by
Fr Ashley Beck

*All booklets are published thanks to the
generous support of the members of the
Catholic Truth Society*

CATHOLIC TRUTH SOCIETY
PUBLISHERS TO THE HOLY SEE

2

Contents

Acknowledgements

Thomas Merton is a writer who still inspires a lot of study and many people know more about him than I do. Among these I am grateful to Paul Pearson, Peter Tyler and Ken Leech for their encouragement and comments, and to Sister Jo Harvey ACI for drawing my attention to the poem about St Paul which concludes the booklet.

Introduction

On the afternoon of 10th December 1968, in a hotel room in Bangkok, a fifty-three year old American monk was electrocuted and killed, probably as a result of touching an electric fan after having a shower. This booklet is an introduction to the life and influence of this man, one of the great spiritual writers of the 20th century and one of the most important figures of North American Catholicism.

In the United States, Merton has not only remained an important figure: a whole cornucopia of research and writing has blossomed since his death. The lists of new material issued regularly by the Thomas Merton Center in Kentucky[1] show that over two hundred pieces of writing – either new editions of his own work, or writings about Merton or inspired by him – are appearing *every year*. One of Merton's major biographers, the late Monica Furlong, was English, although her biography was published in America[2]. The fortieth anniversary of his death, which has been marked by special events in this country[3], gives us an opportunity to reappraise Merton's abiding influence.

Merton's life and writings spanned a period of great renewal and upheaval in the life of the Catholic Church:

what he wrote gives us a picture of this, played out in his own vocation and struggles. While we can see how far he changed and developed, at the same time there is an element of continuity and important points of contact between Merton in 1941 and 1968.

Merton's search for God

The big connecting strand in the whole of Merton's life is also the reason why he remains so important: the place of God in the life of the person and of the world. His long search for God which took him into the Cistercian monastery at Gethsemani was the same search which led him to give such inspiration to American peace activists in the 1960s; his whole life, encompassing so many of the questions which contemporary men and women raise, was a journey towards a fuller relationship with God. But he pursued this search at a time when western culture was becoming effectively 'post-Christian': when Christians of all traditions have had to renew themselves and look at their distinctive beliefs. As Peter Tyler has pointed out, Merton recognised that 'we find ourselves, as Christians, in a return to the conditions of the early Christians – i.e. Christians have once again become a minority within a largely un-Christian majority and cannot rely on secular and political powers to back up their positions, whether theological, moral or political.'[4]

Merton's writings today

Within this context two major and closely related concerns of Merton's writings remain crucial for Christians forty years after his death. First, his writings about contemplative prayer, the critical and prophetic role of the contemplative, drawing on the richness of Catholic tradition and also open to the insights of other Christian communities and world faiths, still need to feed the Church: in the midst of stress and a culture in the western world which has become more manic, more greedy and more self-absorbed since 1968 we need a deep contemplative practice inspired by what Merton wrote and how he lived; moreover there are still false spiritualities at large. Second, the way he applied this 'contemplative prophecy' to the struggle against war and the glorification of war remains inspirational. We may not feel that we live in the shadow of nuclear conflict in the same way, and the Vietnam War seems very distant, but the witness of the Catholic Church and other Christian communities against, for example, the invasion of Iraq in 2003 and the continued possession and upgrading of nuclear weapons by countries like the United States and Britain, show that we still need Merton's teachings. His insights have been influential in changing the Christian environment and in the way in which the Church's Magisterium has addressed issues of war and peace.[5]

The sources for Merton's life and thought are legion. He wrote an immense amount and seldom seems to have thrown anything away, in spite of doubts in his early life as a monk about whether he should be a writer. Apart from the published material, much of it reworked, we have special insights into Merton's soul from his autobiographical reflections. First, the account of his journey to faith in Christ and the religious life which made him famous, *The Seven Storey Mountain*; many of his early writings on the spiritual life are drawn from journals, and all of them have now been published in several volumes, as have his letters. In a booklet of this kind we can only hope to sketch over some of his writings and introduce the reader to this exceptional man, whose writings are so varied and exciting; I have given a lot of space to direct quotations as he should be allowed to speak for himself.

Monica Furlong begins her biography in these words, which are hard to better: 'I am among those who regard Thomas Merton's life as a victorious one, a life that, although it was cut short by accidental death when Merton was fifty-three, was lived to a rare degree of joy and fulfilment; a life that understood and revealed much about the twentieth century and, in particular, the role of religion within it.'[6]

Merton's Early Life

In the spiritual life we are rightly encouraged to see ourselves as pilgrims and strangers on earth (*advenae*), not tied to particular countries or backgrounds – this is why Christians stand by the refugee and the migrant. The background of Thomas Merton is consistent with this: we think of him as a classic American Catholic, and although he spent periods of his childhood in America, he did not settle permanently there until his twenties and he was in his mid-thirties before he became an American citizen.[7]

His childhood

He was born in the French Pyrenees in the village of Prades on 31st January 1915. His father, Owen Merton, was an artist from New Zealand; his mother Ruth (née Jenkins), from Long Island, New York, was also an artist and the two had met while studying in Paris under the Canadian painter Percyval Tudor Hart. His mother was a very able woman with a streak of perfectionism; as a mother she seems slightly detached and cold.

The family moved to America, near Ruth's family, but tragically when Merton was six years old she was diagnosed with stomach cancer and died: some have suggested that her personality and the manner of her death had a psychological effect on him affecting his future religious vocation: she told him she was going to die by means of a letter. Many years later he remarked: 'Perhaps solitaries are made by severe mothers.'[8]

On the move

This trauma was bound to engender a sense of rootlessness; so was what happened next. Owen Merton needed to support Thomas and his younger brother John Paul but as an artist this was bound to be insecure. In the next few years the family moved around various parts of France and back to America, with the boys often left with relatives or at boarding schools. At the same time these early experiences had a positive effect: appreciation of art and the beauty of creation, an early knowledge of French and Spanish and a healthy scepticism about accepted values in society. Although his father had some links with the American Episcopalian Church the practice of religion seems to have played little part in his childhood life, although during his periods living in France he saw glimpses of Catholic life.

As the 1920s progressed his mother's family, particularly his grandparents and aunts, played a bigger role in his upbringing and in his early teens Thomas settled in England and he went to Oakham School in Rutland. Although at the time this was seen as a lower to middle-ranking public school academically, it was at Oakham that Merton's intellectual and literary ability first flowered, and he edited the school magazine. His father also died, after a long and painful illness, in 1931. From this point Merton's godfather, and old friend of his father's from New Zealand, Tom Bennett, became his legal guardian: Bennett was a Harley Street doctor with a sophisticated French wife. Their influence gave the young Merton confidence in not accepting the accepted *mores* of English upper middle-class society at that time. As Furlong puts it: 'As he began to explore London by himself, and so move away from the safe havens of Ealing and Rye [where his relatives lived] he began to feel horror at the poverty and decadence that underlay the pin-neat, Gilbert and Sullivan façade, to detect a brutality that frightened him and a terrible desolation that touched his own deepest wounds.'[9] Later he wrote of 'Men in bowlers and dark suits...with their rolled-up umbrellas. Men full of propriety, calm and proud, neat and noble.'[10] This sense of critical detachment from affluent society never left him; it also made him very negative about living in England, although he did first in London encounter the work of William Blake, which was very influential upon him.[11]

Cambridge and leaving England

The intellectual formation he received at Oakham paid off and in 1933 he went up to Gonville and Caius

College, Cambridge, to read Modern Languages. We might be inclined to see this as a good and positive thing, but for Merton the experience of being a student at one of the foremost universities in Europe was almost entirely negative and even destructive. Intellectually he found the place unstimulating and from his own account led a dissolute life in what was his first and only year. He had a love affair with a woman and fathered a child by her.[12] At the end of the academic year, having accumulated debts, his godfather Tom Bennett told him he would have to leave Cambridge; Merton returned to the United States (never to visit England again, although he was intending to go to England and Wales on his way back from Asia at the time of his death) and enrolled at Columbia University in New York. Although he kept in touch with English relatives and was undoubtedly affected by Britain's role in the Second World War[13], his relationship with this country, although formative, was in many ways ambivalent.

Conversion and Entry to the Trappists

Merton began his studies at Columbia in January 1935, a bustling and modern university compared to Cambridge, and a place where he felt much more at home. He came under the influence of Mark Van Doren, who was teaching 18th-century English literature – Van Doren's love of literature and his intellectual sharpness made a deep impression on him; his directness affected his own teaching style later on. Also at this time he dabbled in Communism and got involved in contemporary political causes such as the Italian invasion of Abyssinia. He blossomed intellectually and took courses in Spanish, German and French Renaissance literature.

In *The Seven Storey Mountain* he gives a vivid picture of how empty his life was, at a certain level, but slowly this began to change as he studied medieval French literature and read Etienne Gilson's book *The Spirit of Medieval Philosophy*. This opened up for him a completely new concept of God – 'Aseitas – simply means the power of being able to exist absolutely in virtue of itself...'[14] Hitherto, under the influence of members of his family, he had seen Catholicism as something rather odd and sinister: suddenly now

Christianity made intellectual sense, and he began to go to the Episcopalian church where his father had once played the organ. By the time of this third year at Columbia he had formed a very close network of friends, to whom he remained close for the rest of his life; among the group's intellectual interests was Oriental mysticism, something which held Merton's interest for the whole of his life.

"Father, I want to become a Catholic"

After graduating in 1938 Merton started a master's degree focussing on William Blake, applying to Blake the aesthetic ideas of St Thomas Aquinas, as interpreted by the French Catholic writer Jacques Maritain. Under their influence he learnt, as Furlong puts it, that 'art is part of a mystical and contemplative understanding of the world, that man's passions must be transfigured by love if men are not to prey cruelly on one another, and that men should seek the state of "virtue" in which that transformation has taken place or is in the process of taking place. It came to Merton that, child of his age that he was, he had tried to interpret life in terms of sociological and economic laws, but that these separated from faith and charity became yet another form of imprisonment.'[14a] This realisation changed him very deeply – he wanted to devote himself to mystical union with God. What might surprise us is that initially he combined this enthusiasm with a lifestyle not normally linked to this aspiration – smoking heavily, pursuing girls and getting drunk (although he seems to have talked about mysticism in his cups). He began, however, to go to Mass in a Catholic Church, Corpus Christi church on the edge of Harlem in New York. In order to immerse himself in a Catholic atmosphere he read the works of Gerard Manley Hopkins and (surprisingly) James Joyce. One night the desire to become a Catholic became irresistible; he was reading correspondence between Hopkins and John Henry Newman:

'Suddenly, I could bear it no longer. I put down the book, and got into my raincoat, and started down the stairs. I went into the street. I crossed over and went along by the gray wooden fence, towards Broadway, in the light rain. And then everything inside me began to sing… I had nine blocks to walk. Then I turned the corner of 121st Street, and the brick church and presbytery were before me. I stood in the doorway and rang the bell and waited. When the maid opened the door, I said: "May I see Father Ford, please?" "But Father Ford is out."… The maid closed the door. I stepped back into the street. And then I saw Father Ford coming around the corner from Broadway… I went to meet him and said: "Father, may I speak to you about something?" "Yes," he said, looking up, surprised. "Yes, sure, come into the house." We sat in the little parlour by the door. And I said: "Father, I want to become a Catholic."'

On 16th November 1938 he was baptised and made his First Holy Communion; his godfather was visiting professor at Columbia, Dan Walsh, who lectured on Aquinas and Duns Scotus, and another seminal influence on Merton and a lifelong friend. In his autobiography Merton describes the experience: 'Now I had entered into the everlasting movement of that gravitation which is the very life and spirit of God. God's own gravitation towards the depths of His own infinite nature, His goodness without end. And God, that center Who is everywhere, and whose circumference is nowhere, finding me... And He called out to me from His own immense depths.'

Although he later regarded his early period as a Catholic as rather lukewarm most of us would be inclined to think of him as pious – frequent weekday Mass, Confession and Communion, spiritual reading and Stations of the Cross. Having finished his MA on Blake he went on to work on a PhD on Hopkins; he also wrote part of a novel[15], some book reviews and poetry (something he had never been able to do before he became a Catholic).

He records one incident when his non-Catholic friends seemed to have grasped better than he the importance of holiness; in this dialogue his Jewish

friend, Robert Lax says to him: '"What you should say"
– he told me – "what you should say is that you want to
be a saint." A saint! The thought struck me as a little
weird. I said: "How do you expect me to be a saint?"
"By wanting to," said Lax, simply. "I can't be a saint," I
said, "I can't be a saint." And my mind darkened with a
confusion of realities and unrealities: the knowledge of
my own sins, and the false humility which makes men
say that they cannot do the things that they *must* do…
All these people were much better Christians than I.
They understood God better than I. What was I doing?
Why was I so slow, so mixed up, still, so uncertain in my
directions and so insecure?'

"Make me a priest"

The autumn of 1939, when war came to Europe, brought
a new sense of seriousness to Merton and his friends and
it was at this point that the thought suddenly came into
his mind that he was going to be a priest. He made a
resolution during a Novena in St Francis Xavier Church
on 16th Street, before the monstrance: 'Yes, I want to be
a priest, with all my heart I want to be a priest. If it is
Your will, make me a priest – make me a priest.'

He began to go to Mass every day and enquired about
joining the Franciscan Order; he was told he could enrol
in the novitiate the following August. Merton's
personality was characterised by great enthusiasm, and in

this spirit he threw himself into preparing himself for the religious life, teaching himself, for example, *The Spiritual Exercises of St Ignatius Loyola*. He also made an important visit to Cuba, his first experience since his conversion of a Catholic country. But after a few months his vocation to be a Franciscan came to an end, partly because he felt obliged to 'come clean' about the whole of his past dissolute life – as a result he was advised to withdraw his application. He felt enormous pain at this rejection; but it is clear that he had nurtured a rather romantic view of the religious life – that was an illusion which had to be stripped away. Another thing which was perhaps too 'comfortable' about his attraction to the Franciscans was their big involvement in the USA at that time in teaching – indeed after his rejection he got a job teaching at St Bonaventure College in Olean, New York state. It would have been so easy for someone with Merton's gifts for teaching and writing to fit into that environment. But would it bring *this man* closer to God? Was it really demanding enough?

He started to live at St Bonaventure's and became more self-disciplined in his life; among his friends and acquaintances it had become known that he wanted to be a priest, and this changed his relationships. It was by now late 1940 and he was also affected at this time by the bombing of London.

Retreat at Gethsemani

In early 1941 he was told by his friend Dan Walsh of the Trappist monastery at Gethsemani, near Louisville in Kentucky, and he decided to make a retreat for Holy Week and Easter there. 'As soon as I thought about it, I saw this was the only choice. That was where I needed to go.' As he prepared to go he worked on novel-writing,[16] and learnt something about the Trappists and the life of the hermit (which were, of course, not the same thing). This filled him with excitement and at one point he said to the first Franciscan friar he encountered, 'I am going to a Trappist monastery to make a retreat for Holy Week.' The friar said, 'Don't let them change you,' to which Merton replied 'It would be a good thing if they did change me.'

The experience of the retreat did change him – he drank in the whole atmosphere and the rigorous, simple life of prayer. He later wrote: 'The eloquence of the liturgy was even more tremendous: and what it said was one, simple, cogent, tremendous truth: the church, the court of the Queen of Heaven, is the real capital of the country in which we are living. This is the center of all the vitality that is in America. This is the cause and reason why the nation is holding together. These men, hidden in the anonymity of their choir and their white cowls, are doing for their land what no army, no congress, no president could ever do as such: they are winning for it

the grace and protection and the friendship of God.'
When he returned to St Bonaventure's he was unsure
what to do; as an alternative to conventional religious life
he began to work in one of the poorest parts of Harlem in
New York with Baroness Catherine de Hueck[17] and
seriously considered working there permanently – but the
vocation to priesthood, and the effect the Trappist
community had had on him, would not go away. His
friend Mark Van Doren indicated that the fact that Merton
had let the vocation drop when he was rejected by the
Franciscans might be a sign that he had a vocation after
all – and shortly after he concluded, 'The time has come
for me to go and be a Trappist.' He asked to go to
Gethsemani to make a retreat at Christmas, but in effect
had decided to stay there as he got rid of his few
possessions: he was also in danger of being 'called up'
into the armed forces, and in that December of 1941 the
Japanese bombed Pearl Harbour, bringing America into
the Second World War.

Novitiate

He made the journey to Kentucky; after a few days in the
guest wing polishing floors he was accepted into the
novitiate and clothed in white robes – as Merton had
remarked of a new novice he saw on his first visit to the
abbey: 'The waters had closed over his head, and he was
submerged into the community. He was lost. The world

would hear of him no more. He was drowned to our society and become a Cistercian.'

In the 1940s Cistercian communities, particularly in the United States, were noted for extreme simplicity and austerity. The monks wore medieval habits in which they slept; they spent a considerable amount of time in church singing the offices, and what time was left was mostly spent in manual labour; the diet was also very frugal and lacking in protein. One thing everyone knows about Trappists is that they do not speak: silence is kept except when communicating with superiors, although an elaborate system of sign language has been developed.

Merton's first few years in the community were devoted to formation and the various stages leading to full profession as a monk – he was given the name Maria (which they all had) Louis. At the end of 1944 his brother John Paul came to visit him before going off to Europe to serve as pilot in the war and in the course of his visit he received instruction and was baptised into the Catholic Church; shortly afterwards he was killed in France. Merton was a gifted poet, and one of his most moving poems is this tribute to his brother:

'Sweet brother, if I do not sleep
My eyes are flowers for your tomb;
And if I cannot eat my bread,
My fasts shall live like willows where you died.

If in the heat I find no water for my thirst,
My thirst shall turn to springs for you, poor traveller…'[18]

From an early stage in his life as a monk Merton faced
the question of how far he could continue as a writer –
did he want to? Was it not part of his old life? He was
asked to write for the order – booklets about the order to
mark the century of the abbey's foundation. He had
always kept journals and it was on the basis of them that
he decided to write an autobiographical account of this
life, leading to his becoming a Trappist, *The Seven Storey
Mountain*, which became a best-seller.

Ordination and first Mass

His ordination to the priesthood in May 1949 was a point
in his life and a development of immense significance,
bringing forth great and passionate enthusiasm from him.
Here he is writing of his first three Masses as a priest, and
many a priest today will be able to relate to these words:
'In the end I had the impression that all who came to see
me were dispersing to the four corners of the universe
with hymns and messages and prophecies, speaking in
tongues and ready to raise the dead because the fact is
that for three days we have been full of the Holy Ghost
and the Spirit of God seemed to be taking greater and
greater possession of all our souls through the first three
Masses of my life, my three greatest graces. It is all

unfamiliar to me. These graces belong to an apostolic order that are beyond my experience. Yet I cannot say, without ingratitude and stupidity, that they were outside my vocation since they were in a sense its crown. I mean the crown of this portion of my history – of the last seven years. I was brought here for this. For this I came into the world... Day after day I am more and more aware how little I am my everyday self at the altar: this consciousness of innocence is really a sense of replacement. Another has taken over my identity, and this other is a tremendous infancy. I stand at the altar – excuse the language: these words should not be extraordinary – but I stand at the altar with my eyes all washed in the light that is eternity, as if I am one who is agelessly reborn.'[19] Later he wrote about priesthood in these terms: 'The priest is called to be another Christ in a far more particular and intimate sense than the ordinary Christian or the monk. He must keep alive in the world the sacramental presence and actions of the Risen Saviour. He is a visible human instrument of the Christ who reigns in Heaven...'[20]

Merton the Contemplative

The Seven Storey Mountain was a phenomenal success. For someone who had scarcely had anything published before, who had taken the striking step of joining a very strict religious community in which people were not allowed to speak to each other, this early experience of fulfilment as a published author – something denied to many – was both encouraging and disturbing. In his journals Merton is open about his ambivalence: on the one hand he is pleased that his story is being told, and told to a very wide readership (the book sold 50,000 copies in its first year of publication; after nearly sixty years it remains in print), and on the other as a monk in a strictly enclosed order he questions from this early stage whether he should be writing for publication at all. In the Cistercian order at that time there was very little tradition of monks publishing their works: in his early years at Gethsemani Merton was expected to pursue much more limited aims. His growing fame as a writer did not entirely dispel these feelings of unease among Merton's fellow monks and superiors, even though book royalties were signed over to the abbey. In examining his writings about contemplative prayer, we need to remember the personal context for him: this context was a search for a solitary life within the community at Gethsemani, a conviction that he was called to the life of a hermit. Merton's journals and letters show that this was not an easy progress as he met considerable resistance from authorities within the order. In the end it happened and by 1966 he was living in his own hermitage in the abbey grounds; moreover he had established the principle that the life of a hermit was to be an accepted part of Cistercian communities, and others followed his example (including some who had earlier opposed him, such as his abbot, Dom James Fox). In a sense Merton's whole life was a search for God within the experience of solitude. During most of this time he also had a major position of responsibility in the monastery, that of Master of Novices. The number of men coming into the community each year was still large: Merton was a gifted and sensitive teacher, and many surviving members of the community today received their earliest formation from him.

Seeds of contemplation

Shortly after *The Seven Storey Mountain* came out in 1949 Merton published a collection of writings about contemplative prayer, entitled *Seeds of Contemplation*.[21] This drew on his experiences as a novice in the community, but in these years (and indeed later on) Merton felt a deep ambivalence about his writings. When

the original version of *Seeds of Contemplation* appeared
to general acclaim in 1949 and a reviewer called it a
'streamlined *Imitation of Christ*' he was horrified and
wrote: 'God forgive me. It is more like Swift than
Thomas à Kempis. The Passion and Precious Blood of
Christ are too little in the book – only hinted at here and
there. Therefore the book is cold and cerebral.'[22] The
book was reissued in 1961, with much added material.
Merton's genius lies in his remarkable ability to apply to
the needs of ordinary men and women the insights drawn
from the untypical experiences of a Trappist monk.

Merton as a contemplative

The Second Vatican Council's constitution on the Church,
known by the Latin title *Lumen Gentium*, broke what was
in many ways new ground by stressing that all baptised
Christians – not just clergy and religious – were called to
live holy lives. In many ways Merton's writings in the
1950s about contemplative prayer – along with those of
other writers – anticipated this call. But it is important to
remember that Merton, like so many of us, was constantly
'feeling his way' in his prayer life – his journals and other
writings show difficulties he had. For example, he did
have difficulty with liturgical prayer in common with
others, even after many years of living in community. It
might have been the aesthetics of the surroundings (this
was before the Abbey church was reordered in the 1960s),

but this extract from his journal, contrasting praying the office with others in the church and praying the office in the woods alone might strike a chord with many people today: 'Once again – the Office is entirely different in its proper (natural) setting, out from under the fluorescent lights. There Lauds is torpor and vacuum. Here it is in harmony with all the singing birds under the bright sky. Everything you have on your lips in praising God is there before you – hills, dew, light, birds, growing things. Nothing in the liturgy of light is lost.'[23]

Merton developed as a contemplative. In the late 1950s one thing which had clearly shifted was his view of the rest of the world, the rest of the human race. If his early writings were characterised by a judgemental attitude towards the world he had left behind him when he became a monk, we can see things change at this pivotal event in 1958, the 50th anniversary of which has recently been commemorated. Merton had been on a visit from the monastery to the nearby town of Louisville. On 19th March 1958 he wrote: 'Yesterday, in Louisville, at the corner of 4th and Walnut, suddenly I realised that I loved all the people and that none of them were or could be totally alien to me. As if waking from a dream – the dream of my separateness, of the 'special' vocation to be different. My vocation does not really make me different from the rest of men or put me in a special category except artificially, juridically. I am still a member of the human race, and what more glorious destiny is there for men, since the Word was made flesh and became, too a member of the Human Race!'[24] This famous passage recalls one of the chapters in *Seeds of Contemplation*, 'Everything that is, is Holy', in which Merton writes: 'Detachment from things does not mean setting up a contradiction between "things" and "God" as if God were another "thing" and as if His creatures were His rivals... The saint knows that the world and everything made by God is good, while those who are not saints either think that created things are unholy, or else they don't bother about the question one way or another because they are only interested in themselves.'[25] This is fundamental to his vision of what contemplative prayer is about. If it reflects contempt for others or for the created order, it is not genuine; nor can it be an escape from these things, from the world in which we live.

What is contemplation?

He opens *Seeds of Contemplation* with some definitions of what contemplation is, and what it is not. 'Contemplation is the highest expression of man's intellectual and spiritual life. It is that life itself, fully awake, fully active, fully aware that it is alive. It is spiritual wonder. It is spontaneous awe at the sacredness of life, of being. It is gratitude for life, for awareness, and for being...contemplation reaches out to the knowledge and even to the experience of the transcendent and inexpressible God. It knows God by seeming to touch Him. Or rather it knows Him as if it had been invisibly touched by Him... Contemplation is also a response to a call: a call from Him who has no voice, and yet who speaks in everything that is, and who, most of all, speaks to us in the depths of our being: for we ourselves are words of His.'[26] Again, slightly later on: 'Nothing could be more alien to contemplation than the *cogito ergo sum* of Descartes, "I think, therefore I am". This is the declaration of an alienated being, in exile from his own spiritual depths, compelled to seek some comfort in a *proof of his own existence* based on the observation that he "thinks"... He is reducing himself to a concept. He is making it impossible for him to experience, directly and immediately, the mystery of his own being. At the same time, by also reducing God to a concept, he makes it impossible for himself to have any intuition of the divine reality which is inexpressible...'[27] In other words, the Christian trying to engage in contemplative prayer is at odds with the prevailing culture and its assumptions – we try to enter a new and different realm of reality. This message is so important: many popular forms of spirituality do not question the self-centredness and individualism of western culture, but rather twist the Christian religion to fit into this mould.

Distractions in prayer

But Merton's writings are not simply theoretical: there is much practical advice, aimed at all readers. So the chapter 'Learn to be alone'[28] contains good advice about finding the right setting for contemplative prayer: 'There should be at least a room, or some corner where no one will find you and disturb you or notice you. You should be able to untether yourself from the world and set yourself free, loosing all the fine strings and strands of tension that bind you... Once you have found such a place, be content with it, and do not be disturbed if a good reason takes you out of it. Love it, and return to it as soon as you can, and do not be too quick to change it for another. City churches are sometimes quiet and peaceful solitudes, caves of silence where a man can seek refuge from the intolerable arrogance of the business world. One can be more alone, sometimes, in church than in a room in one's own house. At home, one can always be routed out and disturbed (and one should not resent this, for love sometimes demands it). But in those quiet churches one remains nameless, undisturbed in the shadows, where there are only a few chance, anonymous strangers among the vigil lights, and the curious impersonal postures of bad statues. The very tastelessness and shabbiness of some churches make them greater solitudes, though churches should not be vulgar. Even if they are, as long as they are dark it makes no difference.' Many a priest has heard penitents confess to distractions in prayer, and Merton devotes a whole chapter to this. 'Prayer and love are really learned in the hour when prayer becomes impossible and your heart turns to stone. If you have never had any distractions you don't know how to pray. For the secret of prayer is a hunger for God and for the vision of God, a hunger that lies far deeper than the level of language or affection. And a man whose memory and imagination are persecuting him with a crowd of useless or even evil thoughts and images may sometimes be forced to pray far better, in the depths of his murdered heart, than one whose mind is swimming with clear concepts and brilliant purposes and easy acts of love. That is why it is useless to get upset when you cannot shake off distractions...'[29] He goes on to point out that the energy we often expend trying to get rid of the distractions creates 'a nervous tension which only makes everything a hundred times worse.' This does not mean that they are not a problem – 'there is considerable danger that our meditation will break down into a session of mental letter-writing or sermons or speeches or books or, worse still, plans to raise money or to take care of our health.' Some of this arises from how overloaded people's lives are: people are often too active, and it might be necessary to cut down the pressure of work.

The nature of Christ

Merton's approach is rooted in belief in the Incarnation of Christ. He describes the 'mystery of Christ in the Gospel' as being like a magnifying glass: 'Through the glass of his Incarnation He concentrates the rays of His divine Truth and Love upon us so that we feel the burn, and all mystical experience is communicated through the Man Christ. For in Christ God is made Man. In Him God and man are no longer separate, remote from one another, but inseparably one, unconfused and yet indivisible... The normal way to contemplation is a belief in Christ that is born of thoughtful consideration of His life and His teaching...' He grapples with the problem of our use of imagination – a problem if we superimpose our own picture of Christ onto what we see in the gospels – and comes back to the patristic concept of the union in Christ's person of his divine and human natures, as taught in the fifth-century Councils of Ephesus and Chalcedon.[30] This vision remains important. Christian spirituality which is not rooted in orthodox Christology, right beliefs about the nature of Christ, will not bear fruit in an authentic union with God; nor will it lead to 'right practice', *orthopraxis*, in the way we live our lives or try to transform the life of the world. So often, even within the Catholic tradition, the full implications of the doctrine of the Incarnation are set aside or viewed as irrelevant: what Merton shows is how our lives of prayer and contemplation have to be grounded in what we assert about the nature of Christ. He links this too to the concept of participation in God, *theosis*, found in eastern theologians of the early Church such as St Gregory of Nyssa; we are led to mystical union with God through the Incarnation.

Traditionally one of the safeguards of right beliefs about Christ is the place we give to Mary, portrayed by the Fathers of the early Church as *theotokos*, 'God-bearer', Mother of God. So Merton's chapter in *Seeds of Contemplation* 'The Woman Clothed with the Sun'[31] shows his deep love for her. '... To love her and to know her is to discover the true meaning of everything and to have access to all wisdom. Without her, the knowledge of Christ is only speculation. But in her it becomes experience because all the humility and poverty, with which Christ cannot be known, were given to her. Her sanctity is the silence in which Christ alone can be heard, and the voice of God becomes an experience to us through her contemplation.'

Love in solitude

It is belief in the Incarnation as the root of contemplative prayer which leads Merton to assert – in a way which was striking in the 1950s and which challenges many people today – that the true contemplative is also a prophetic critic of injustice in the world. Distance from the world when we seek union with God is not a way of escaping from the world or of looking down on it. As the Anglican writer Ken Leech has put it, 'Merton saw solitude and solidarity as interconnected.'[32] Merton wrote that the practice of solitude brings 'a deepening awareness that the world needs a struggle against alienation. True solitude is deeply aware of the world's needs. It does not hold the world at arm's length.'[33] In the early journals entitled *The Sign of Jonas* he wrote: 'It is deep in solitude that I find the gentleness with which I can truly love my brothers.'[34] Later he gave this description: 'the dimensions of solitary prayer are those of man's ordinary anguish, his self-searching, his moments of nausea at his own vanity, falsity and capacity for betrayal. Far from establishing one in unassailable narcissistic security, the way of prayer brings us face to face with the sham and indignity of the false self that seeks to live for itself alone and to enjoy the "consolation of prayer" for its own sake. This "self" is pure illusion, and ultimately he who lives for and by such an illusion must end either in disgust or madness.'[35] It was – in his later years – this philosophy of solitude which led Merton to social criticism, to the view of the contemplative and the monk as one who is *wakeful*. If we are really growing in self-knowledge we will be led away from too great a concern for the self; we will also reject the individualism which dominates so much of western culture. As Leech writes, 'Prayer thus liberates us from self, and from all ideas of self.'[36]

Monks as social critics

In *Contemplative Prayer* and in the lecture Merton gave in Bangkok on the day he died he portrays the monk as one who 'belongs to the world, but the world belongs to him insofar as he has dedicated himself totally to liberation from it in order to liberate it.'[37] Consequently the monk has to speak out against injustice precisely because of his vocation to prayer and reflection, to the stripping away of false illusions in his own life. It is because the monk is on the margins of society that he is given the opportunity for real discernment; although this view is developed most fully in the writings from the last decade of his life, we can see very early signs of it. When he was first exploring the idea of a vocation to the religious life in the early 40s, what put him off some orders was that all they seemed to be doing was teaching – they seemed to occupy far too comfortable a role within American Catholicism, and this included the Franciscan order (to which he was attracted). Since so many orders have now withdrawn from teaching in the years since Vatican II, we can see how Merton's vision of the religious as someone marginalised has, at least in part, been vindicated – he saw monks as 'people who have consciously and deliberately adopted a way of life which is marginal with respect to the rest of society, implicitly critical of that society, seeking a certain distance from that society and a freedom from its domination and its imperatives, but nevertheless open to its needs and in dialogue with it.'[38]

In his writings on contemplation Merton applies this criticism by embracing the life of the poor and in reflections about war and hatred.[39] In our next chapter we will look at the latter priority in more detail as it became a major theme of his writings.

Merton the Peace-Maker

Merton's developed vision as a contemplative led him, in articles and written works, to address many social and political issues in the 1960s. He was closely associated with Dorothy Day and the *Catholic Worker* communities from the late 1950s and these communities' commitment to the poor[40]; he also wrote about racial issues in the 1960s. But there is one issue above all which is associated with his teaching and in relation to which he has had a lasting influence – not only because of his commitment to it, but because he was disgracefully prevented from writing about it: Christian teaching about war and peace. In addition to Day, Merton was close to the Jesuit priest Daniel Berrigan who has also written about Merton's influence on him and the role of contemplative prayer in the Church's struggle against war.[41] Forty years after his death, in a world which is very different from that of 1968, this remains one of the most significant and original contributions he made to the life and teaching of the Catholic Church and the whole of Christianity, the more so because of the pain he experienced through being silenced. Now as then, this issue is at the centre of Christian identity in relation to the world. The outlooks which attempted to justify American militarism and the bomb in the early 1960s are still with us: they are still used to mislead people into thinking that nuclear weapons offer some sort of security; used in the past against the Russians, they are now applied to the Muslim world.

The 1950s

We have seen how in the 1950s Merton progressed from a disdain for the world, expressed so clearly in the way in which he wrote about his original vocation to the religious life in the Trappist community in Gethsemani, to a more positive love of humanity and a commitment to dialogue with the world, a concept made more real in the teachings of Vatican II. But this shift, for him as for the whole Church, should never be seen as an acceptance of ways of living which are inconsistent with the Gospel of Jesus Christ. For Merton in the early 1960s this distinction was at the heart of his teaching.

It is important to recall the context of these years. In some parts of the western world people were beginning to question the morality of possessing nuclear weapons: in Britain, CND had been founded in 1958 and the Labour party had come near to committing itself to unilateral nuclear disarmament. In the United States, while a few voices had claimed that an all-out nuclear war would be immoral, on the whole Catholic bishops and theologians did not question the policies US governments had carried out since the bombing of Hiroshima and Nagasaki which had ended the Second World War, in spite of a much more questioning and negative attitude shown by Pope Pius XII throughout the 1950s. Fidel Castro's revolution in Cuba had made many Americans even more fearful of a Communist invasion than they had been before; there was a widespread climate of fear.

War and peace

Merton's teachings about war and peace were grounded in his theology. As Leech has pointed out, violence is rooted in the view that evil cannot be reversed – the authentic Christian view is that evil can be changed into good by forgiveness and love, and this requires the Christian to have inner peace. So 'Non-violence is not for power but for truth. It is not pragmatic but prophetic. It is not aimed at immediate political results but at the manifestation of fundamental and crucially important truths.'[42]

Thomas Merton's writings about peace and war were published originally in a number of different places and most have been reissued after his death in various collections. One journal he used a lot was the *Catholic Worker*; his first piece in it was a poem, 'Chant To Be Used in Procession Around a Site with Furnaces'. It ended with the words, 'Don't think yourself better because you burn up friends and enemies with long-range missiles without ever seeing what you have done.'[43]

Merton on Nazi 'sanity'

What is it about his writings which makes them, and him, so important? One crucial characteristic is his originality and the way in which he was able to tackle difficult issues imaginatively, drawing on the fairly recent experiences of the Second World War (in which his brother John Paul had been killed in the Air Force flying over Germany). For example, his essay 'A Devout Meditation in Memory of Adolf Eichmann'[44], reflecting on the Nazi mass murderer's trial in Israel, is a profound exploration of Eichmann's *sanity*. Eichmann was not odd: 'He was not bothered much by guilt. I have not heard that he developed any psychosomatic illnesses. Apparently he slept well... Eichmann's sanity is disturbing. We equate sanity with a sense of justice, with humaneness, with prudence, with the capacity to love and understand other people. We rely on the sane people of the world to preserve it from barbarism, madness, destruction. And now it begins to dawn on us that it is precisely the *sane ones* who are the most dangerous. It is the *sane ones*, who can without qualms and without nausea aim the missiles and press the buttons that will initiate the great festival of destruction that they, *the sane ones*, have prepared.'[45] He dwelt on the same theme of normality and ordinariness in 'Auschwitz: A Family Camp'[46] where he dwelt on the trials in Germany of guards from Auschwitz. These men and women considered themselves to be ordinary, respectable people; and yet they committed unspeakable crimes with what seemed to be a clear conscience. The reason that these writings about the Second World War are so important is that Merton linked them with contemporary attitudes – not only (in the Auschwitz piece) with recent killings of civil rights activists in Mississippi in 1964 but with the state's defence policies. The link with World War II is crucial and Merton draws on this in other writings.

Censorship

The scandal surrounding what Merton wrote about war and peace is that after some of the early writings, from 1962, most were banned from publication by the censors and superiors of the worldwide Cistercian order. The precise details are complex[47]; the censorship reflects the widespread ambivalence over these issues in the western world – both the United States and France (where the order is based) – and also a view that a contemplative monk should not write about issues of this kind. Nearly fifty years later we find this incomprehensible and shocking; it reflects so much of the scandalous indifference of so many Catholics towards the danger, then, of worldwide war. This view, though now discredited, has not disappeared completely[48], so it is salutary to recall the real pain that Merton experienced and the great damage that was done to Christian witness by the actions of his superiors.

The timescale of his writings is less important than their overall vision and the disturbing way in which he was silenced. The primary concern which they addressed was the Cold War and the threat of nuclear weapons: the essays still have a freshness which repays reading now, especially in the light of events since Merton's death. The only way to form a good overview is to look at these writings from four angles.

The Original Child Bomb

The first angle from which Merton examines the issue is the history of the Second World War. The bombing of Hiroshima and Nagasaki in August 1945[49] was still a comparatively recent event, and much of Merton's most moving writing reflects on this terrible event. The poetic 'Points for meditation to be scratched on the walls of a cave' entitled 'Original Child Bomb'[50] draws on detail about the weeks leading up to the bombing and the actions of those involved in flying the bomber *Enola Gay*. The power of the piece actually comes from its flat, dead-pan style:

'In the year 1945 an Original Child was born.
The name Original Child was given to it by the
    Japanese people,
who recognised that it was the first of its kind…
… The bomb exploded within 100 feet of the
    aiming point.

The fireball was 18,000 feet across.
The temperature at the center of the fireball
    was 100,000,000 degrees.
The people who were near the centre became nothing.
The whole city was blown to bits and the ruins
all caught fire instantly everywhere, burning briskly.
70, 000 people were killed right away or died
    within a few hours.
Those who did not die at once suffered great pain.
Few of them were soldiers.'

Merton's use of World War II history was not confined
to Hiroshima – we have already referred to his reflections
about Auschwitz. In *Peace in the Post-Christian Era*[51] he
wrote about the ways in which Allied policy during the
war had shifted from a commitment not to bomb civilian
targets to the 'blanket bombing' of cities like Dresden.[52]

'Just War' and nuclear war

But Merton's arguments against nuclear weapons were
not simply subjective; nor were they simply about the
consequences of nuclear attacks.[53] He draws on his deep
knowledge of the Fathers by contrasting the attitudes
towards war of Origen and St Augustine, and analysing in
detail how far the traditional 'Just War' doctrine can be
applied to the intention to use nuclear weapons. For
Merton, Augustine appeared to compromise by accepting

the inevitability of war and conflict, rejected by Origen in his dispute with Celsus – the earlier theologian, like all the earliest Christians, thought the world would end soon, so war for the preservation of the Empire was simply irrelevant, whereas 'Augustine saw the shattered and collapsing Empire attacked on all sides by barbarian armies. War could not be avoided. The question was, then, to find out some way to fight that did not violate the law of love'[54] – hence the development of the Just War doctrine or theory. As is well known, this part of the Catholic theological tradition seeks to contain and limit war by laying down conditions - war only as something defensive, as a last resort, waged by a properly constituted authority, and the avoidance of the deliberate killing of the innocent, of non-combatants. As with the conventional bombing of German and Japanese cities during World War II, for Merton, as for others[55], this is the crucial moral and theological argument against both the use – ever – of nuclear weapons and their possession with the intent to use them, the basis of the whole theory of nuclear deterrence. The deliberate killing of innocents is never permitted; the use of these weapons would always entail that deliberate killing; therefore their use and the intent to use them is not permitted – these arguments are still crucial. In our own day they are the basis of the criticism of nuclear deterrence policies in the *Compendium of the Social Doctrine of the Church*[56] and the even stronger condemnation of them as 'fallacious' by Pope Benedict XVI.[57] Merton is less clear about practical ways of responding to this immorality – he does not simply endorse a 'unilateralist' position (in the same way, although defending and expressing his admiration for Dorothy Day[58] he does not appear to advocate an absolute pacifist position in the same way as she did). What is striking is that he was not afraid to challenge the compromises being made by American theologians who were less clear in their condemnations of nuclear weapons policies, such as the respected and influential Jesuit John Courtney Murray.[59]

The effects of Communism

A third aspect of his teaching on peace is the way in which he was disturbed at the moral effect of the Cold War on American society. It is perhaps difficult for us to recall how strong people's fears of Communism were fifty years ago but he writes a great deal about how destructive this could be, as in the essay 'Red or Dead? The Anatomy of a Cliché'.[60] He wrote: 'The muddle-headed, frustrated, stubborn and obtuse assumptions that underlie our view of the world and its problems, produces no clarity, only darkness and desperation. Thought becomes more and more rudimentary. We strive to soothe our madness by intoning more and more vacuous clichés...' He analyses how so much thinking in the US at that time led to defeat and despair – it also denied the tradition of democracy which it was supposed be defending. Many have made similar criticisms in our own time about the rhetoric and actions surrounding the 'War on Terror'.

Merton and Nhat Hanh

The final aspect follows from this: as the 1960s developed, the United States was drawn more and more into the Vietnam War, a conflict characterised by both futility, in that it was clear that the USA could not win it, and by terrible incidents of brutality against civilians. The opposition of Pope Paul VI to the conflict (in contrast to the attitude of the American Bishops) was mirrored by that of peace activists in the US such as Dorothy Day and Fr Daniel Berrigan SJ. Merton was clearly linked to this group and gave retreats for those engaged in peace work.[61] He also had contacts with Vietnamese monks as part of his dialogue with Buddhism and wrote about one of them, 'Nhat Hanh is My Brother'[62] – he was a Buddhist monk who was working for peace and reconciliation in the midst of the war: 'He represents the least "political" of all the movements in Vietnam. He is not directly associated with the Buddhists who are trying to use political manipulation in order to save their country. He is by no means a Communist. The Vietcong is deeply hostile to him. He refuses to be identified with the established government which hates and distrusts him. He represents the young, the defenceless, the new ranks of youth who find themselves with every hand turned against them except those of the peasants and of the poor, with whom they are working. Nhat Hanh speaks truly for the people of Vietnam, if there can be said to be a "people" still left in Vietnam.' In the United States ignorance of Vietnam and its culture was widespread – in arguing against the war and the mentality of fear behind it Merton was trying to dispel that ignorance. It can be argued that we face today an analogous situation with regard to the world of Islam.

More censorship and the death of John XXIII

In 1962 Merton was refused permission by the authorities of the Cistercian Order to publish the essays in *Peace in a Post-Christian World*. Some of his works on the issue of peace were published in various ways at about this time, sometimes anonymously, but by this stage the order would not even allow the re-issue of material published earlier. In his journals and letters Merton gives vent to his pain and strong sense of injustice, and to the way in which his vow of obedience as a monk was proving very costly in terms of what was a life and death issue. The situation did not really change until the rules for censorship within religious orders were changed after the Second Vatican Council.

The supreme irony about the way Merton was treated by his superiors is that the things he was trying to write were the subject of the last and greatest encyclical of Blessed John XXIII. In *Pacem in Terris*,[63] published in Holy Week 1963, not long before his death from cancer, the pope issued the strongest possible condemnation of modern warfare, seen as 'mad', *alienum a ratione*. If anything the pope's condemnation is more forthright than Merton's writings, and Merton writes that it was good that there weren't Cistercian censors in the Vatican. He was very moved by the pope's last few days and death: 'Pope John is dying and perhaps dead. Already yesterday at this time he was in a coma, in an oxygen tent, with the papal guards around his apartments. Last night he was conscious for a moment, they say, and smiled and blessed those around him. I have been thinking of him all day and praying for him.'[64]

Closing Years and Death

The last years of Merton's life in the 1960s were marked by his frustrated work for peace in the midst of war and fear. By this stage he was living almost entirely in his hermitage in the forest near the abbey at Gethsemani. Alongside this solitude, or yearning for solitude, he nevertheless had contact by letter with major figures elsewhere in the world. Two encounters give a flavour of this: he corresponded by letter from the late 1950s with the Russian writer Boris Pasternak; not altogether flippantly he points out in his journals similarities between a writer living in an oppressive state and a censored monk[65]; he also corresponded with Henry Miller. Another encounter, at a later stage, was the visit to his hermitage of the singer Joan Baez.

Changes and decisions

During and after the Second Vatican Council Merton was deeply involved in the renewal of religious life ushered in by the Council in its decree *Perfectae Caritatis*. This led the community at Gethsemani to look at its whole life, and many trivial aspects of community life which Merton had found increasingly unhelpful were discarded. The abbey's communal worship was also renewed, and Merton welcomed much of this; he did not, however, welcome all changes uncritically and he thought many rather superficial.

One volume of his journals from the period covering 1966 has been named by his editors *Learning to Love*. This is because during a stay in hospital Merton fell in love with a student nurse; for the rest of that year their friendship developed into something much stronger and Merton was faced with an agonising choice between this relationship and his vocation. Perhaps it was not really a choice as he seems in his journals to rule out completely ceasing to be what he was – a celibate priest – but the depth of the couple's mutual love is very clear. Contact gradually came to an end.

Psychology, knowledge and God

There are two further aspects of Merton's teachings which flowered in his closing years and remain important. The first was his positive view of contemporary insights in psychology. The English academic Peter Tyler has pointed out 'Merton was one of the first Christian writers to make accessible a bridge between the psychological and theological enterprises.' In his writings about contemplation Merton teaches that the created 'self' has to disappear: 'The unitive knowledge is not a knowledge of an object by a subject, but a far different and transcendent kind of knowledge in which the created 'self' which we are seems to disappear in God and to know him alone. In passive purification then the self undergoes a kind of emptying and an apparent destruction, until, reduced to emptiness, it no longer knows itself apart from God.'[66] This parallels Carl Jung's search for the 'authentic self' though 'individuation'. Authentic Christian spirituality needs to draw on the best of contemporary psychological and psychotherapeutic insights, and Merton's reflections are a valuable resource for this.

Interfaith dialogue

Probably better known is Merton's exploration of the spirituality of other religious faiths. He studied Hasidism and Sufism,[67] he wrote passionately about Mahatma Gandhi[68] and his writings on Zen Buddhism – particularly in the light of the Vietnam War – opened up a new tradition to many western readers. What was it that interested him? Leech writes: 'It was in Zen that he rediscovered the need to transcend the western divisions of matter and spirit, subject and object. In order to progress to God-consciousness, it is necessary to lay aside discursive reasoning and thought, and to go beyond the thinking process to the centre of Being itself.'[69] Both at this level, and in terms of meditative techniques, Merton broke new ground for Catholics in terms of inter-faith dialogue and the ways in which we can learn from different traditions; in the 1960s he was also engaged in contacts with Christians from other traditions, such as the German theologian Karl Barth, who was to die on the same day as Merton in 1968; he was also influenced by the Lutheran pastor Dietrich Bonhoeffer.

Above all a tradition of monasticism helped him realise how much monks from different religions had to learn from each other, and what they could all do to teach the world. This growing interest led to the last journey of his life. He was offered the opportunity to travel to Bangkok in Thailand at the end of 1968 for a big international conference on monasticism. It was agreed that he would travel elsewhere *en route*, giving talks and visiting other communities.

Last Mass

Merton had a great devotion to the 'Apostle of the Slaves', the Jesuit St Peter Claver, and his friends in the community here describe him celebrating what turned out to be his last Mass at Gethsemani, in honour of the saint: '... Father Louis read the beautiful Gospel narrative of the Good Samaritan, after which he surprised us with a brief but deeply moving homily. He compared himself to "the traveller" who had been attacked by robbers and was then left half dead along the road, and described how we each in our own way had been Good Samaritans to him, helping him "to get out of the ditch." He embarrassed us by expressing his appreciation for all we had done for him (precious little it was) and he said he was offering the Holy Sacrifice of the Mass for our intentions.'[70]

Merton and the Dalai Lama

The highlight of the journey was Merton's meeting in India with the spiritual leader of Tibetan Buddhism, the Dalai Lama, in early November. He wrote: 'I like the solidity of the Dalai Lama's ideas. He is a very consecutive thinker and moves from step to step. His ideas of the interior life are built on very solid foundations and on real awareness of practical problems. He insists on detachment, and on an 'unworldly life'; yet he sees it as a way to complete understanding of and participation in the problems of life and of the world. But renunciation and detachment must come first…'[71] This description of a man who is still one of the great spiritual leaders in the world (who has since met many Catholic leaders) reiterates much of Merton's own teaching about contemplative prayer. The Dalai Lama said of Merton: 'When I think of Christians I think of Thomas Merton.'

His last day

Merton gave a lecture at the conference in Bangkok on the morning of 10th December, on 'Marxism and Monastic Perspectives'. In this he explored the notion of dialogue between the monk and the Marxist, drawing on the thought of Marcuse. He pointed out that the monk 'belongs to the world, but the world belongs to him insofar as he has dedicated himself totally to liberation from it in order to liberate it' and his own aim was 'to keep alive the contemplative experience and to keep the way open for modern technological man to recover the integrity of his own inner depths.'[72]

After the lecture Merton joked with photographers, expressed a wish for a Coke, had lunch and went to the cottage he was occupying in the hotel grounds for a siesta. The other Trappist delegates to the conference wrote to the Abbot of Gethsemani of what happened next: 'Not long after he retired a shout was heard by others in his cottage, but after a preliminary check they thought they must have imagined the cry. He was found at the end of the meridian (afternoon rest) and when found was lying on the floor. He was on his back with the electric fan lying across his chest. The fan was still switched on, and there was a deep burn and some cuts on his right side and arm. The back of his head was also bleeding slightly... It is believed he could have showered and then had a heart attack near the fan, and in falling knocked the fan over against himself; or again that being in his bare feet on a stone floor he may have received a fatal electric shock...in his death Father Louis' face was set in a great and deep peace, and it was obvious that he had found Him Whom he had searched for so diligently.'[73]

With irony which would not have been lost on Merton, his body was collected by the US Army and flown back to the United States in one of their military transport planes used to bring soldiers back from Vietnam, and he was buried in Gethsemani on 17th December.[74] In his journals he had expressed a wish to be home for Christmas, and indeed he was.

'When I was Saul'

This booklet has been published during the special Year of St Paul, intended to help Christians reflect on the importance of the Apostle to the Gentiles; so it is fitting to conclude with this poem about St Paul by Thomas Merton, which shows well his mastery of English and his religious imagination:

'When I was Saul, and sat among the cloaks,
My eyes were stones, I saw not sight of heaven,
Open to take the spirit of the twisting Stephen.
When I was Saul, and sat among the rocks,
I locked my eyes, and made my brain my tomb,
Sealed with what boulders rolled across my reason!

When I was Saul and walked upon the blazing desert
My road was quiet as a trap.
I feared what word would split high noon with light
And lock my life, and try to drive me mad:
And thus I saw the Voice that struck me dead.

Tie up my breath, and wind me
   in white sheets of anguish,
And lay me in my three days' sepulchre
Until I din my Easter in a vision.

Oh Christ! Give back my life, go, crass Damascus,
Find out my Ananias in that other room:
Command him, as you do, in this my dream.'

Further Reading

Merton's output was prodigious and it is not possible to list here (or perhaps anywhere on earth) everything he wrote. He once wrote that he was like Peter Pan, for helping to construct a posthumous existence for himself, and was aware of the contradictions implicit in keeping and preserving nearly everything he ever wrote.[75] Many essays are to be found in various different collections, and Merton revised some of his early work; some of his writings from the early 60s about peace have only been published comparatively recently because he was censored by the authorities of the Cistercian order. The United States remains the centre of most published studies and other research. Translations of his work into various world languages are being made all the time.

The International Thomas Merton Society and the Thomas Merton Center in Bellarmine University in Louisville, Kentucky (*www.merton.org*) are vital sources of information and have custody of the archival material, including unpublished writings entrusted to the Center by Merton before his death. There is also a Thomas Merton Collection at St Bonaventure's College, Olean, where Merton taught before he became a monk. *The Merton Seasonal* is a quarterly publication produced jointly by the Center and the ITMS. The Thomas Merton Society in Britain and Ireland (*www.thomasmertonsociety.org*) organises events in this country and publishes twice a year The Merton Journal; it is responsible for the Thomas Merton Collection of books housed at the Catholic Central Library at St Michael's Abbey, Farnborough.

What follows is a selection of the most important works by Merton himself and about him. Producing any kind of bibliography for a writer like Merton carries the risk of leaving out something important; some publications in England are only to be found in second-hand bookshops.

Merton's own work

Thomas Merton *The Seven Storey Mountain* (London: Sheldon 1975) This is the American original published in 1949. An abridged edition, edited by the novelist Evelyn Waugh (with Merton's approval), was published in England at the time of the original publication, entitled Elected Silence (London: Burns and Oates 1949) It leaves out some material thought at the time to be of interest only to American readers.

The Sign of Jonas (London: Sheldon 1976)

Bread in the Wilderness (Tunbridge Wells: Burns and Oates 1974)

Seeds of Contemplation (Wheathampstead: Clarke 1961), originally published as New Seeds of Contemplation and a revision of a much earlier work with the same title published in 1947.

Peace in the Post-Christian Era ed. Patricia A. Burton (Maryknoll: Orbis 2004) This is the book not published in 1962 because of the actions of the authorities of the Cistercian order.

The Intimate Merton His Life from His Journals ed. Patrick Hart and Jonathan Montaldo (Oxford: Lion 2000) The entire text of the journals, in seven volumes, has been published by Harper (*Born in the Mountains, Entering the Silence, A Search for Solitude, Turning Toward the World, Dancing in the Water of Life, Learning to Love* and *The Other Side of the Mountain*).

The Letters of Merton have been selected and edited in various volumes, under the titles *The Courage for Truth, The Hidden Ground of Love, The School of Charity* and *Witness to Freedom*; also *Selected Letters* ed. David Cooper (New York: Norton 1997)

Raids on the Unspeakable (New York: New Directions 1966)

No Man is an Island (London: Burns and Oates 1955)

Contemplative Prayer (London: Darton, Longman and Todd, 1973)

On Peace (London: Mowbrays 1976)

Conjectures of a Guilty Bystander (London: Sheldon 1977)

The Collected Poems of Thomas Merton (New York: New Directions 1977)

Contemplation in a World of Action (Notre Dame: University of ND Press, 1998)

Passion for Peace ed. William Shannon (New York: Crossroad 1995)

Essential Writings selected by Christine M. Bochen (Maryknoll: Orbis)

Mystics and Zen Masters (New York: Farrar, Strauss, Giroux, 1967)

Zen and the Birds of Appetite (Kentucky: The Abbey of Gethsemani, 1968)

Biographies and studies

Michael Mott *The Seven Mountains of Thomas Merton* (Boston: Houghton Miffin 1984)

Monica Furlong *Merton: A Biography* new ed. (Liguouri: Liguouri Press 1995)

Jim Forest *Living With Wisdom A Life of Thomas Merton* (Maryknoll: Orbis 1991)

Hart, Patrick OCSO (ed.) *Thomas Merton, Monk* (London: Hodder and Stoughton 1974)

Joan Chittister OSB 'Thomas Merton Icon of the Voice of God', in *A Passion for Life Fragments of the Face of God* (Maryknoll: Orbis 1998)

Kenneth Leech 'Contemplation and Resistance as seen in the Spirituality of Thomas Merton', in *The Social God* (London: Sheldon 1981) pp. 39ff.

Ronald F. Powaski *Thomas Merton on Nuclear Weapons* (Chicago: Loyola 1988)

Peter Tyler 'Thomas Merton forty years on: a post-modern guide for troubled times' *The Pastoral Review* vol. 4 issue 6 (November/December 2008) 'A Spirit of Optimism: Thomas Merton and a Christian Spirituality for a New Millennium', *The Pastoral Review* vol. 2 issue 4 (September/October 2006) 'Thomas Merton: Ikon of Commitment to the Postmodern Generation', *The Way* Supplement 98 (2000)

End notes

[1] Listed quarterly in *The Merton Seasonal* published by the Center, at Bellarmine University in Louisville, and the International Thomas Merton Society.

[2] New ed., Liguori: Liguori publications, 1995.

[3] Such as a gathering on 10th December 2008 in London addressed by Dr Paul Pearson from the Merton Center and the Anglican Archbishop of Canterbury, Dr Rowan Williams.

[4] 'Thomas Merton forty years on: a post-modern guide for troubled times', *The Pastoral Review* vol. 4, issue 6 (November/December 2008), p. 36.

[5] As we shall see his writings about peace which were censored by his order in the early 1960s said the same things as Blessed John XXIII's great encyclical *Pacem in Terris* (CTS S264). We can see the same common mind with the highest authorities in the Church in respect of Pope Paul VI's opposition to the Vietnam War, so undermined by Cardinal Spellman and the American hierarchy. The consistent denunciation of modern warfare by the Servant of God, Pope John Paul

II, and the teachings of Pope Benedict XVI on nuclear weapons, show how far this tradition has developed, and Merton's courageous witness is part of this.

[6] Op.cit., p. xiii.

[7] Furlong op.cit., pp. 173ff.

[8] The Sign of Jonas (London: Sheldon 1976), quoted in Furlong p. 14.

[9] Op.cit., pp. 44-45.

[10] My Argument with the Gestapo (New York: Doubleday 1969, reprinted by New Directions, 1975).

[11] He later wrote: '... Through Blake I would one day come, in a round-about way, to the only true Church, and to the One Living God, through His Son, Jesus Christ.' (The Seven Storey Mountain [London: Sheldon 1975], p. 88. His father had always had a devotion to Blake; Merton was later to teach Blake at St Bonaventure University.

[12] This delicate subject is side-stepped in The Seven Storey Mountain, but seems to have been a reason why the Franciscans would not accept him as a novice. The poignancy of the affair was increased by the fact that the mother and child were killed during the Blitz.

[13] He wrote in October 1940: 'Today I saw a movie of London under bombing and heard the recorded sound of the air raid alarm and of the all-clear signal. For the first time in my life, I think, I momentarily wanted to be in the war' (The Intimate Merton, ed. P. Hart and J. Murtando [Oxford: Lion 1999], p. 39). It was momentary, since by the end of the year he had submitted papers to the US authorities making clear his conscientious objection to taking up arms in any war which the USA might enter: this process affected the timing of his eventual going to Gethsemani.

[14] The Seven Storey Mountain, p. 172 (quotations in this chapter are from this work, unless otherwise noted.)

[14a.] Furlong, op. cit. p. 71.

[15] Straits of Dover, also known as The Night Before the Battle and The Labyrinth (unpublished, held at the Thomas Merton Center).

[16] See Furlong pp. 91ff. for details; the only one to have survived was My Argument with the Gestapo (New York: Doubleday 1969).

[17] 'Friendship House' was a lay community which provided support for local people in a way similar to the Catholic Worker houses founded by Dorothy Day and Peter Maurin.

[18] *Thirty Poems* (New York: New Directions 1944). The poem continues:

> 'Where, in what desolate and smokey country,
> Lies your poor body, lost and dead?
> And in what landscape of disaster
> Has your unhappy spirit lost its road?
>
> Come, in my labor find a resting place
> And in my sorrows lay your head,
> Or rather take my life and blood
> And buy yourself a better bed –
> Or take my breath and take my death
> And buy yourself a better one.
>
> When all the men of war are shot
> And flags have fallen into dust,
> Your cross and mine shall tell men still
> Christ died on each, for both of us.
> For in the wreckage of your April Christ lies slain,
> And Christ weeps in the ruins of my spring:
> The money of Whose tears shall fall
> Into your weak and friendless hand,
> And buy you back to your own land;
> The silence of Whose tears shall fall
> Like bells upon your alien tomb.
> Hear them and come: they call you home.'

[19] *The Intimate Merton* p. 90.

[20] 'Vocation', in *No Man is an Island* (London: Burns and Oates 1955), p.125.

[21] Ed.

[22] *Ibid*., p. 87.

[23] *The Intimate Merton* p. 225.

[24] *The Intimate Merton* pp. 150-160. The place where this happened has been remamed 'Merton Square.'

[25] *Seeds of Contemplation* (Wheathampstead: Anthony Clarke, 1961), pp. 17ff and *passim*.

[26] Pp. 1-3.

62

[27] Pp. 6-7.
[28] Pp. 62ff.
[29] Pp. 171ff.
[30] Pp. 117ff.
[31] Pp. 131ff.
[32] 'Contemplation and Resistance in the Spirituality of Thomas Merton' in *The Social God* (London: Sheldon 1981), p. 42. I am indebted to the insights of this essay in this section.
[33] *Conjectures of a Guilty Bystander* (London: Sheldon 1977), p.10.
[34] P. 268.
[35] *Contemplative Prayer* (London: Darton, Longmad and Todd 1973), pp 25-26.
[36] *Op.cit.*, p. 44.
[37] *The Asian Journal of Thomas Merton* (London: Sheldon 1974) p. 341.
[38] Cited in George Woodcock, *Thomas Merton, Monk and Poet* (Edinburgh: Canongate 1978), p. 117f.
[39] *Seeds of Contemplation* 'He who is not with Me is against Me', pp. 137ff. and 'The Root of War is Fear', pp. 86ff.
[40] *Passion for Peace*, ed. William T. Shannon (New York: Crossroad 1995), contains many pieces originally written for the *Catholic Worker*. For an account of the paper and the movement see Ashley Beck, *Dorothy Day* (CTS B 705).
[41] See, for example, *America is Hard to Find* (London: SPCK 1971). Berrigan knew Merton well and his writings have remained important, such as his application of the Lamentations of Jeremiah to the attacks on the World Trade Centre in New York in 2001, *Lamentations* (London: Sheed and Ward 2002).
[42] *Raids on the Unspeakable* (New York: New Directions 1966) p. 22.
[43] *Catholic Worker* July/August 1961, quoted in R. Ellsberg (ed.) *The Duty of Delight The Diaries of Dorothy Day* (Milwaukee: Marquette University Press 2008), p. 316 note 206.
[44] Originally published in *Raids on the Unspeakable* (New York: New Directions 1966), also in *On Peace* (London: Mowbrays 1976, pp. 82ff.)
[45] Pp. 82-83.
[46] *Ibid.*, pp. 72ff.

[47] See the introductory essays by Forest and Burton in *Peace in the Post-Christian Era* (Maryknoll: Orbis 2004)

[48] For an examination of how 'Neo-Conservatives' in the American Catholic community, such as Michael Novak and George Weigel, attempted to undermine Catholic opposition to the 2003 invasion of Iraq, using similar arguments as those used to muzzle Merton, see William Cavanaugh, 'To Whom Shall We Go?' in D. L. O'Huallachain and J. Forrest Sharpe (eds.) *Neo Conned! Just War Perspectives: A Condemnation of War in Iraq* (Vienna, Va.:.IHS Press 2005), pp. 269ff.

[49] See J. Siemes SJ, *The Day the Bomb Fell* (CTS S 373) and Ashley Beck, *Dorothy Day*, pp. 45ff. and *Ronald Knox* (CTS B 710), pp.44ff.

[50] Originally published in 1962 and reprinted in *On Peace* pp. 7ff.

[51] Maryknoll: Orbis 2004, pp. 58ff.

[52] At the time virtually the only Christian leader in Britain to question the bombings was the Anglican Bishop of Chichester, George Bell. See R.C.D. Jasper, *George Bell* (London: OUP 1987).

[53] One of the most important critiques of nuclear weapons theory, J. Finnis, J. Boyle and G. Grisez, *Nuclear Deterrence, Morality and Realism* (Oxford, Clarendon Press 1987) is critical of bishops and others whose arguments are largely 'consequentialist' – Merton is not guilty of this.

[54] 'War in Origen and St Augustine' in *Peace in the Post-Christian Era*, p.41.

[55] For example the English Catholic philosopher Elizabeth Anscombe (a supporter of Day and the Catholic Worker movement) in Walter Stein (ed.) *Nuclear Weapons and Christian Conscience* (London: Merlin 1961), a book to which Merton refers. See also Finnis, Boyle and Grisez, *op.cit.*

[56] London: Continuum 2005.

[57] Message for World Peace Day 2006.

[58] *Peace in the Post-Christian Era* p. 151.

[59] 'Theologians and Defense', *ibid.*, pp. 75ff.

[60] Pp. 121ff.

[61] For details of one see Leech, *op.cit.*, p. 45. He was, however, very distressed by the suicide outside the United Nations building of the *Catholic Worker* activist Roger LaPorte in November 1965 and

considered severing his links with the peace movement because of this; see *The Intimate Merton* pp. 320-1. His reaction caused some distress to Day; for her reaction see Ellsberg, op.cit. p. 374 with note 248.

[62] *On Peace* p. 152, also in *Faith and Violence*.

[63] CTS S 264.

[64] *The Intimate Merton* p. 258.

[65] Ibid. p. 69. On his relationship with Samuel Beckett see Mary Bryden, 'From Writing to Silence', *The Tablet* 13th December 2008, pp. 8ff.

[66] *Art.cit.*, pp. 38ff., quoting *Contemplative Prayer* p. 94.

[67] P. 39, and also 'Sufism and Christianity' in P. Sheldrake (ed.) *The New SCM Dictionary of Christian Sprituality* (London: SCM 2005).

[68] 'A Tribute to Gandhi' in *On Peace* pp. 127ff.; he also edited a book about him, *Gandhi on Non-Violence* (New York: New Directions, 1964). Merton cannot fairly be accused of syncretism in his attitudes to non-Christian religions – he was completely in line with the teachings of the Council and what the Church has done since then. In a radio interview in December 2008 Dr Rowan Williams pointed out that Merton's spirituality never ceased to be based on faith in the Trinity; this gave him confidence to learn from other religions (BBC Radio 4, *Something Understood*, 14th December 2008).

[69] *Op.cit.*, p.48.

[70] Patrick Hart OCSO (ed.) *Thomas Merton, Monk A Monastic Tribute* (London: Hodder and Stoughton 1974), Prologue, p. 16.

[71] *The Intimate Merton*, p. 422.

[72] *The Asian Journal of Thomas Merton* (London: Sheldon 1974) quoted in Leech, *op.cit.*, p. 46. In discussions about the life of the monastery in Kentucky Merton was suspicious about the effects of modern agricultural technology on the life of the monks.

[73] Letter in the Thomas Merton archives quoted in Furlong, pp. 312-313.

[74] The obituary by Dorothy Day in the *Catholic Worker* (December 1968), 'Thomas Merton, Trappist: 1915-1968', dispels rumours that he had been contemplating leaving the monastery with evidence from his letters (Ellsberg, *op.cit.*, p. 432, note 288)

[75] *The Intimate Merton*, introduction, 'A Path through Thomas Merton's Journals', p. 14.